Sport Diving

To Dr. B. H. Salvat, Directeur de l'Antenne du Muséum National d'Histoire Naturelle et des Hautes Etudes en Polynésie Francaise, and his colleagues—Dr. Alain Sournia, Dr. Jean Pierre Renon, Dr. René Galzin, Dr. Jean Jaubert, Yves Polvêche, and Dr. Michel Ricard—with deep appreciation for their friendship and good will during our exploration of the islands and atolls of French Polynesia

ACKNOWLEDGMENTS: All of the photographs in this book have been provided by Carter M. Ayres except for the following: pp. 7, 15, 20, 23, 27, 36, 37, Dr. Richard Boyd; pp. 10, 11, Greg Sutter; p. 29, Dick Schewe; p. 33, Greg Kent; p. 41, Carole S. Briggs. For their assistance in the preparation of this book, the author and the photographer wish to thank Beth Somermeyer and her associates, The Gordon Flesch Company, Inc.; Dr. Richard Boyd, Petries SCUBALAB; Professor Alfred C. Glauser, University of Wisconsin; Willie Winter, Greg Sutter and Jeff Scott Olson, all of Madison, Wisconsin; Greg Kent, Bill Steinborn, Dick Schewe, and the members of the Rockford Divers Association, Rockford, Illinois.

Editorial Consultant: Dr. Richard Boyd

Superwheels &
Thrill Sports

Sport Diving

CAROLE S. BRIGGS

Photographs by
CARTER M. AYRES

Lerner Publications Company ■ Minneapolis, Minnesota

LIBRARY OF CONGRESS CATALOGING IN PUBLICATION DATA

Briggs, Carole S.
Sport diving.

(Superwheels & thrill sports)
SUMMARY: Describes sport diving using SCUBA equipment and discusses basic techniques, safety tips, and good dive sites.
1. Scuba diving—Juvenile literature.
[1. Scuba diving. 2. Diving] I. Title. II. Series.
GV837.6.B74   797.2'3   82-35
ISBN 0-8225-0503-7   AACR2

Manufactured in the United States of America

International Standard Book Number: 0-8225-0503-7
Library of Congress Catalog Card Number: 82-35

1 2 3 4 5 6 7 8 9 10 91 90 89 88 87 86 85 84 83 82

CONTENTS

INTRODUCTION **6**

A HISTORY OF SCUBA **8**

LEARNING TO DIVE **11**

DIVING EQUIPMENT **15**
Surface Equipment *17*
SCUBA Equipment *18*
Accessories *26*
Cameras *29*

DIVING SAFETY **31**
The Buddy System *31*
The Effects of Water Pressure *31*
"Plan Your Dive and Dive Your
    Plan" *32*

A TYPICAL DIVE CLUB **34**

PEOPLE IN DIVING **35**

EXPLORING THE CORAL REEF **39**

CONCLUSION **46**

INTRODUCTION

Beneath the surface of any body of water—lake, river, or ocean—lies a world unknown to anyone who has never been SCUBA diving. Self-Contained Underwater Breathing Apparatus (SCUBA) was invented in 1943 by the French diver Jacques-Yves Cousteau because he wanted more freedom for underwater exploration. Now it is used by research and sport divers around the world.

Diving can be done in the chilly lakes of the midwestern United States or in the clear warmth of oceanic coral reefs. Some people dive with just one friend, while others prefer to dive with many people and join dive clubs that offer a variety of underwater activities.

If you live near a lake, diving can mean a Saturday or weekend outing with friends or family. Many divers also spend their vacations diving at exciting island resorts such as Grand Cayman in the Caribbean, Bonaire off South America, or Heron Island on Australia's Great Barrier Reef. Dive shops and clubs may sponsor these trips with the aid of travel agents who arrange both your flights and your stay at special diving resorts where diving equipment and boats are available.

In California, divers can see giant kelp beds—seaweed that grows to 80 feet in size—and, along the Kona Coast in Hawaii, they can explore beautiful coral reefs. Some divers like to explore old shipwrecks in the Great Lakes, while others love to identify the many colorful and varied fish that abound in all of the world's oceans. For experienced divers in the Midwest, ice diving with a team of divers and surface crew can be both thrilling and demanding. In much the same way, divers in Florida explore underwater caves with special equipment and techniques. But whatever your interest or wherever you dive, underwater exploration with SCUBA can be a very exciting sport.

A diver exploring the wreck of the freighter *America* tries to turn a steam control valve inside the ship. The *America* went down in Lake Superior in 1928 when it struck submerged rocks during a foggy night.

A HISTORY OF SCUBA

Until 1943, if people wanted to explore the ocean they had to wear huge, lead-weighted boots, copper diving helmets (out of which they could hardly see), and canvas suits coated with rubber, which looked like baggy space-suits. They received air from a long hose extending from the diver to an air pump on the surface. Because they were restricted by the air hose, divers had to stay quite close to shore or a boat.

The early diving suits did not protect divers from the cold, and they were also awkward to move around in. During shallow dives, the air trapped inside the suits kept divers afloat. Then when divers succeeded in getting below the surface, the air compressed as they descended, making them so heavy that they ended up lying in the sand at the bottom instead of being able to walk around. Sometimes the air rushed to the bottom of their suits, flipping divers upside down.

Despite the many advances that were made in conventional diving technology, before 1943 divers were always encumbered by their heavy gear and their dependence on surface men and machinery for air. That year French Navy officer Jacques-Yves Cousteau created a diving revolution when he made diving gear that was both lightweight and self-contained. With his co-inventor, engineer Emile Gagnan, Cousteau invented the Aqualung.

An aqualung—or SCUBA as it is now called—has two main parts: a tank of compressed air and a combination of valves and hoses that allow the diver to breathe. As the diver inhales, air is fed automatically from the tank into the diver's mouth and lungs. As the diver exhales, the regulator releases the "used" air into the surrounding water. The tank is strapped to the diver's back and, although it may weigh as much as 40 pounds on land, it is almost weightless in the water. Thus the diver can move about with the weightless ease of a fish, independent of the surface. Cousteau and Gagnan's aqualung freed divers to explore and work in a way that was previously impossible.

Later, Cousteau also designed a rubber wetsuit to minimize the effect of cold on the submerged diver. The wetsuit fitted the body just snugly enough to allow a thin layer of water to become trapped between the diver's body and the rubber suit. This thin film of water, warmed by the diver's body heat, acts as an insulator against the surrounding water.

Since then, manufacturers of diving equipment have increasingly catered to the safety and the comfort of the diver. Today, divers may choose from a variety of tanks, regulators and wetsuits unheard of during Cousteau's first SCUBA sea trials. And excellent opportunities to learn diving skills, including underwater safety, are available from certified diving instructors in most parts of the country.

French marine biologist Dr. Jean Jaubert collects a coral sample 150 feet below the surface on a coral atoll.

Dr. Dick Boyd includes something from the history of sport diving as he conducts a basic certification class. The old-fashioned two-hose regulator he demonstrates was designed by Jacques-Yves Cousteau.

LEARNING TO DIVE

Most divers begin their training through the YMCA or through a local dive shop that sponsors lessons. Training takes place in a swimming pool and in a classroom. After about 30 hours of instruction, including final tests, the new diver will get his or her *basic certification.*

Before you can enroll, many courses require that you be able to swim 25 yards under water without coming up, tread water for 10 minutes, and do the crawl or freestyle for at least 200 yards. Others simply make sure that you are comfortable in the water. You don't have to be an expert swimmer, but the better you are, the safer diving will be for you.

In the typical classroom session, the instructor introduces each piece of equipment and explains how it works. The classroom lessons will also cover in detail the effects of water pressure on divers and the rules that must be followed for safe diving.

SCUBA instruction manuals stress safety as the most important aspect of all diving operations.

At the same time, divers begin pool lessons. First they work with only the mask, fins and snorkel, but soon they progress to using the SCUBA equipment. Students learn ways to enter the water wearing their gear, how to share compressed air with another person, how to relieve the pressure on their ears as they descend, and how to come up correctly from the bottom. Many courses also include techniques for rescuing disabled divers.

In this pool lesson, diving students are required to put on their equipment while under water. These exercises, called ditch and recovery, help build a diver's confidence.

At the end of the course, students are required to take a written examination to test their classroom knowledge, a pool exam to test their skill in using the equipment, and three open-water dives to introduce them to diving in an actual lake or ocean. In the open-water dives, the class will descend to a depth of about 30 feet. The instructor will ask to see each diver clear his or her mask of water and will also probably ask each diver to remove his or her tank pack and put it on again. This exercise helps new divers to feel comfortable with their equipment. The instructor will also watch each new diver ascend to the surface to make sure he or she does it properly. Assuming the class is able to do all of these maneuvers (most people do pass), each is given a card that includes his or her photograph. This basic certification card allows divers to join dive club expeditions, to have tanks filled with air, and to rent equipment at resorts. People who don't have certification cards don't have access to air and equipment, so the chances of people diving without proper training are greatly reduced.

Divers who have their basic certification and feel confident as open-water divers often take advanced classes. These classes teach compass reading and other skills for night diving, ice diving, cave diving, wreck diving, and underwater photography. Some divers become so interested in the sport that they decide to continue their training and get an instructor's rating. As an expert, they can then lead groups of less experienced divers on all kinds of interesting diving expeditions—old sunken ships, coral reefs in the Caribbean, and ice dives.

An ice diver is about to enter the water. Below the surface, the temperature of the water is only slightly colder than it is during the summer, and the visibility is much better. To assure that the diver will not lose the hole in the ice, he holds onto a rope during the dive. The rope is tended at all times by someone on the surface.

This diver's mask is designed specifically for use with the unisuit he is wearing.

DIVING EQUIPMENT

Because humans can only breathe under water if they have special equipment, proper selection and care of equipment is very important. Divers must be able to depend on each piece of equipment and know enough about it to keep it in good working order.

15

This diver is wearing wetsuit boots with full-foot fins.

SURFACE EQUIPMENT

The first items a diver will acquire are the mask, fins, and snorkel. These three pieces of equipment are also used (without SCUBA equipment) to *skin dive,* or snorkel. Snorkeling is fun in shallow riverbeds and lakes and even in pools.

Face Masks. Face masks fit over the eyes and nose. A face mask fits well if it stays in place when you put it on your face without the strap and inhale through your nose. Although everything looks one-third larger under water, people who require eyeglasses or contact lenses may need to get a mask with special vision-correcting lenses. After all, the whole point of diving is to see what's under water!

Fins. Fins come in two types—*full-foot* fins and *heel-strap* fins. Full-foot fins fit just like shoes. They are lightweight and are good for beginners or for diving in calm, fairly shallow water. Strap fins are like half of a shoe with a strap in the back that holds the fin to your foot. They are made of heavier rubber and are larger. To give a snug fit and to prevent the fin from rubbing against the foot, socks or wetsuit boots are worn with strap fins. On small feet, it also works well to wear tennis shoes inside the fins. Because they are stiffer, the heel-strap fins propel divers through the water better than the full-foot types.

Snorkel. A snorkel is a tube which allows someone to breath with his or her face in the water. The best snorkels have wide breathing tubes with few bends and have a comfortable mouthpiece. Never use a snorkel with the ping-pong ball device in the tube. Designed to keep the water out, the ball can actually trap water in the breathing tube. The snorkel is always worn on the left side of the face mask, attached by a *keeper,* or figure eight-shaped piece of rubber. That way, it doesn't interfere with the regulator, which is worn on the right side.

These student divers practice helping each other put on their gear.

SCUBA EQUIPMENT

In addition to the masks, fins, and snorkel, divers use other equipment. Some of the items are necessary and others just make diving more fun.

Tank and Regulator. The compressed air tank is, of course, essential for underwater breathing. Some divers rent tanks already filled with air from dive shops; other divers own tanks and have them filled at the shop. Most divers prefer aluminum tanks because they do not rust and have a very long life expectancy.

Tanks come in different sizes. The larger tanks are heavier but will hold more air, allowing the diver to remain under water longer. The most popular size is the 80-cubic-foot tank, which holds 3,000 pounds per square inch (p.s.i.) of air. This tank will allow the average diver to stay at 30 feet for approximately an hour. By federal law, the inside of the tank must be subjected to water pressure in excess of its 3,000 p.s.i. rating to test the strength of its walls every five years. This process, called *hydrostating,* should only be done in an authorized test facility since a weak tank could explode.

Some tanks are equipped with *J-valves,* which hold back a reserve of air. The J-valve cuts off the diver's air gradually as the pressure in the tank drops to 300 p.s.i. When a diver using this kind of tank notices that it is becoming harder to breathe, he or she pulls the rod that controls the valve, and the reserve supply of air becomes available. At this point, the diver must return immediately to the surface.

Many tanks, however, have another kind of valve called a *K-valve,* which operates like a water faucet. When the K-valve is open, the diver gets air. When the air supply has been used up, the diver gets no air. Divers who use tanks equipped with K-valves must also use a

The needle in this pressure gauge points to zero, which in this case indicates that the air has not yet been turned on. While not in use, both the gauge and the second stage, the round chrome piece directly below the gauge, are piled on top of the tank to prevent damage.

pressure gauge that tells them how much air remains in their tank at any given time.

The mechanism that attaches to the tank valve is called the *first stage.* It reduces the pressure of the air in the tank from about 120

An ice diver exits the water through a triangular hole. His tank is topped by a J-valve. Hoses attached to the valve lead to the regulator, the pressure gauge, and the dry suit.

to 140 p.s.i. Several hoses can be attached to the first stage. One hose will connect the first stage to the *second stage.* Both stages together form the regulator. This is the piece of equipment that fits in the mouth and allows the diver to breathe under water. The regulator contains a *demand valve,* which opens when the diver breathes in to give the diver exactly the right amount of air. When the diver breathes out, the used air flows out through two exhaust pipes and into the water. These are the bubbles you may have seen in photographs or movies of divers. Since the regulator supplies air from tank to diver,

The regulator hose is usually worn so that it comes over the right shoulder.

it must be of good quality and kept free of dirt, sand, and water. It should be checked periodically for stiff or nonworking parts by a good dive shop.

The *pressure gauge* is attached to the tank by a hose in the same way that the regulator is attached. Some divers also carry a second demand regulator, also connected by hose to the first stage. This regulator, known as an *octopus* or a *safe second*, is carried solely for the purpose of safety. It can be used if the first regulator malfunctions. Or, if one of the divers runs out of air, two divers can both breathe off the same tank until they reach the surface. Octopuses are standard gear for wreck, cave, and ice divers, since immediate ascent to the surface is not always possible if equipment malfunctions.

Buoyancy Compensator. Another necessary piece of equipment is the buoyancy compensator, or BC as most divers call it. This is an inflatable vest that helps the diver control his or her buoyancy, so the diver can remain at one depth without rising or sinking. The BC comes in handy on the surface, too, since a totally inflated BC keeps the diver afloat without treading water. To add air to the BC, the diver blows into it through an oral inflator. To descend, the diver must let air out of the BC. Some BCs are equipped with automatic inflators which connect the BC to the air in the tank. With an automatic inflator, the diver pushes one button to add air to the BC and another to release air. Some BCs have a built-in tank pack. Divers who don't use these BCs wear backpacks to hold only their tanks.

Wetsuit. For diving in any water colder than 75°F (about 24°C), a full wetsuit is essential. Short wetsuits are usually worn during warm water dives. Since our bodies maintain a temperature of 98.6°F (37°C), water cooler than that drains away body heat. Although a diver may not feel cold in warm water, the body must work to maintain its temperature or the diver will tire quickly.

This woman is skin diving in a clearwater springs in Florida. Since they breathe through the snorkel, skin divers spend most of their time on the surface and only take short dives. This diver wears heel-strap fins with wetsuit boots and a weight belt to offset the extra buoyancy that her short wetsuit provides. The BC gives her an added measure of safety.

Two divers prepare for a lake dive. Both wear full wetsuits, complete with hoods and gloves. Their weight belts, gold in color, show below the orange BCs.

Wetsuits are made of rubber with tiny air cells, coated with nylon. They are available in several thicknesses, ranging from 1/8- to 1/2-inch. For warmer water like Florida and the Bahamas, 1/8-inch suits are ideal. While they insulate the body from cold, they are also less cumbersome than thicker suits, and they don't cause the diver to overheat on the surface. A 1/4-inch wetsuit is necessary for diving in northern lakes, even in the summer. This is because water below 30 feet often stays at 40°F (4-5°C) all year around, even in the summer. Lake divers should also wear wetsuit boots and hood and gloves of the same thickness as the wetsuit. Cumbersome as they are, it is unwise to dive without a hood because much body heat is lost through the head.

A wetsuit should fit snugly at the shoulders, crotch, and underarms, almost like a second skin. Otherwise, as the diver submerges, large pockets of cold water will collect in the suit. Very tall, very short, stocky, or thin people may need a custom wetsuit, one made to fit them exactly.

Higher quality suits are made of rubber coated with nylon on both the inside and outside. This prevents them from tearing on rocks or sharp pieces of coral.

Because the material in a wetsuit contains tiny air cells, it will cause the diver to float unless he or she wears a *weight belt*. A weight belt looks exactly like it sounds—a nylon web strap with several lead weights strung on it. How much weight a diver needs depends on his or her particular body structure. Larger people, for example, usually need to carry more weights than smaller people because a larger person has more body fat and floats more easily. All weight belts should have a buckle that enables the diver to release the belt simply by pulling. For safety, divers wear the belt outside of all other gear so they can remove it quickly in an emergency.

ACCESSORIES

A *depth gauge* measures how far under the surface a diver is. Some are worn like wrist watches, while others fit into a console that is attached to the tank. *Pressure gauges* and *compasses* are also housed in these consoles.

A *dive watch* is waterproof and designed to withstand water pressure at depths of 150 feet and below. Many watches have a ring encircling the face that the diver uses to calculate "bottom time," the amount of time a diver is under water.

There are also *bottom timers* on the market which automatically start when submerged below a few feet and stop again when the diver reaches the surface. It is important for divers to know both how deep they are and how long they have been at that depth.

Many divers carry *knives* strapped to their legs. Knives are useful for prying up rocks or cutting seaweed, and they can be essential if the diver becomes entangled in something.

For night dives or for cave dives, each diver should carry an *underwater light*. A good light will have a sturdy, pressure-resistant case and will be powered by four D-sized dry cells or nickel cadmium batteries.

It's also a good idea to own a special *diver's flag,* which is solid red with a white stripe running from the upper left corner to the lower right corner. Attached to an inner tube above the dive site, it warns people in boats to stay at least 100 feet away. A boat propeller or the keel or centerboard of a sailboat can cause serious injury to the surfacing diver.

These divers are fully equipped to explore Florida's Peacock Springs system. The diver on the right has a yellow console which houses a pressure gauge, a depth gauge, and a compass. Both divers carry underwater lights on their wrists.

This underwater photographer uses a camera housed in aluminum.

CAMERAS

Equipment for underwater photography can be simple or advanced, depending on how serious the photographer is. Beginners can put a simple camera in a Plexiglas housing to keep it dry. This housing has a lever on the outside to operate the camera. More advanced single-lens reflex cameras require Plexiglas housings that have several external controls to adjust focus and trigger the camera. For flash pictures, a separate flash unit can also be housed. Much of this equipment is expensive and heavy, but worthwhile to the avid photographer.

There is also a fairly recent amphibious camera that can be taken under water without a housing. This camera is quite small, yet it is very sturdy. Because the lenses can be changed, the photographer can shoot pictures of everything from tiny tube worms to entire seascapes.

All underwater equipment should be washed off with a hose or under a shower after each day's dive. Unwashed equipment that has been in fresh water will begin to smell after one day. If equipment that has been used in salt water is left unwashed, the salt will deteriorate the rubber and attack the metal parts.

A freshwater crayfish smiles for the camera.

These buddies keep in close contact while they explore together.

DIVING SAFETY

THE BUDDY SYSTEM

The first and foremost rule of safe diving is: **Never dive alone. Always dive with a buddy.** Both members of a buddy team must be in each other's sight at all times. In murky water, this will mean swimming very close together, or within touching distance. Some divers use a *buddy line,* a rope that connects them at the wrists. It may seem like extra trouble to keep track of another person while exploring underwater, but it soon becomes second nature. And if a diver's regulator stops working, if he or she becomes ill or gets stuck in a crevice, the benefits of the buddy system become readily apparent!

THE EFFECTS OF WATER PRESSURE

Although we cannot feel it, the air around us exerts 14.7 pounds of pressure on each square inch of our bodies. For every 33 feet that the diver descends underwater, he or she sustains an *extra* 14.7 pounds of pressure per square inch. This pressure can be felt in the eardrums in much the same way as when the cabin of an airplane is pressurized and depressurized during takeoff and landing. Divers must *equalize* the pressure between their heads and the water. Equalizing is done easily by pinching the nose and blowing gently. Divers should only descend further when they feel the pressure lessen.

Increased underwater pressure also changes the density of air that is in the lungs. The air divers breathe from the SCUBA tank compresses as they go deeper. As they begin rising again, the air in their lungs expands. For that reason, divers must remember *never* to hold their breath. A regular flow of air in and out of the lungs will insure that the air doesn't expand beyond the limit of the lungs. Otherwise, the air sacs in the lungs could burst, forcing air into the bloodstream and possibly to the brain, causing very serious injury or even death. Therefore, when heading toward the surface, divers must ascend slowly and breathe normally. A good rule of thumb is for a diver to follow his or her smallest bubbles from each exhalation to the surface. This will slow the ascent to a safe speed.

In addition, compressed air can create other dangers for divers if they are not careful. The air we all breathe is 80 percent nitrogen and 20 percent oxygen. As we go deeper, the increased pressure allows our body to absorb more and more nitrogen. As the diver slowly ascends, the water pressure decreases, and the extra nitrogen is returned to the lungs and exhaled normally. If a diver goes too deep and ascends too fast, however, the extra nitrogen does not have time to be exhaled, and bubbles of nitrogen develop in the body. Most of these bubbles collect in the joints, causing the diver's joints to ache. This *decompression sickness,* called "the bends," is extremely painful. If the bubbles lodge in the brain or spinal cord, they can cause paralysis or death.

"PLAN YOUR DIVE AND DIVE YOUR PLAN"

To avoid decompression sickness, do not dive too deep and do not stay under too long. Sport divers should never go deeper than 100 feet. And the deeper a dive is, the shorter it should be. At 30 feet, a diver can stay down as long as there is air in the tank. But at 60 feet, a diver can stay down safely for only one hour. These are called *no-decompression* dives.

If a diver exceeds the safety time limit at a certain depth, he or she must *decompress.* To decompress, a diver must remain about 10 feet below the surface for a certain amount of time

This diver explores a sunken aircraft in 35 feet of water. The diver has planned a no-decompression dive at a depth of 35 feet for 45 minutes but will monitor his pressure gauge and ascend immediately when his air supply drops below 500 p.s.i.

to allow his or her body to get rid of excess nitrogen. The United States Navy has developed Repetitive Dive Tables to help divers determine how long to stay at certain depths.

Although the safe diver should never need to worry, it is still important to know the location of the nearest medical facility equipped to help divers in case of an accident.

A TYPICAL DIVE CLUB

Once someone is certified as a basic SCUBA diver, diving with a club can be a lot of fun. Most clubs have monthly meetings to plan diving and other social events. After the business meeting, there is often a speaker who narrates slides about such topics as underwater photography techniques, ice diving, various wrecks to dive, and interesting places to travel and dive.

One dive club, the Rockford Divers, is located in Rockford, Illinois. It sponsors many camping-diving trips for the whole family. Everyone brings tents, sleeping bags, dive gear and plenty of food and spends a wonderful weekend picnicking and diving. Rockford Divers also sponsors day trips to sunken ships in Lake Michigan. There the divers explore moss-covered decks and masts of once seaworthy and proud ships that sailed the Great Lakes.

In a less serious vein, Rockford Divers also sponsors an underwater Easter egg hunt every spring. In each plastic egg is the name of a prize. Finders win such items as dive posters and snorkels. Another seasonal event is the annual turkey shoot. Under water, participants try to hit a target with a spear gun. The person who hits a bull's eye wins a turkey.

At the end of the year, there is an awards banquet. Awards are given for such achievements as attending the most dives and contributing the most to the club's activities. There is also an underwater photo contest, in which prizes are given for the best saltwater and best freshwater photographs. Old artifacts and bottles brought up from the depths are also on display. Because this club has such a large membership, it is able to attract well-known speakers and divers. A newsletter announcing major events is published monthly and no diver need ever worry about not having a diving buddy.

Two members of the Rockford Divers Association are beginning the diving season by practicing basic skills in a nearby lake.

PEOPLE IN DIVING

Photographers. Underwater photography, an exciting hobby for some sport divers, is a rewarding career for Ron and Valerie Taylor, a husband-wife team. They have spent most of their lives photographing marine life off Australia's Great Barrier Reef. Their work is sometimes dangerous—they have filmed large predators like the great white shark—and other times very exciting, like filming huge bat-like creatures called manta rays.

Some underwater photographers take pictures for advertising companies. Companies that sell diving equipment like to show their gear being used under water. And since SCUBA is an exciting sport, some companies make their product more noticeable by showing it being used by divers.

Scientists. Recently, marine biologist Dr. Sylvia Earle became the first person to use a diving suit that looked like a robot but allowed her to explore 1,250 feet beneath the surface—

the deepest any single human being has ever been. The suit allowed her to find out which creatures live at such depths without going through the weeks of decompression that would otherwise be necessary from diving so deep. She stayed 2-1/2 hours and found a few fish, some crabs, and even an eel. But her most exciting find was bamboo coral. Approximately six to eight feet high, it looked like sticks of bamboo. When Dr. Earle touched the coral, the stalks began to pulsate with a blue light that moved in rings up and down the length of the creature.

Dr. Dick Boyd operates a dive shop. A specialist in diving science for many years, Dick has a lab for testing new equipment and checking out old equipment for divers. As a dive shop manager, Dick must be familiar with all the latest equipment and how it is used. He teaches several classes each year for beginning and advanced divers and he and his wife sponsor trips for certified divers to

A diver exits the companionway leading to the engine room on the wreck of the freighter *Emperor* in Lake Superior.

dive sites all over the world. The Boyds also have a large sonar-equipped boat, which they use in Lake Michigan to locate shipwrecks that have never been found.

Commercial Divers. Some people earn their living by diving to salvage goods and equipment that have sunk with ships. Others salvage cars that have fallen through the ice or

A wreck diver examines a double block he helped raise from a wreck in Lake Michigan. A decompression meter is strapped to his left wrist.

rolled into lakes during car accidents.

Still other divers are underwater construction workers who help to build offsea drilling rigs for oil companies. For each of these diving jobs, special equipment and skills are needed. Most commercial divers are even "wired for sound" so that they can communicate with workers on the surface.

Moorea is a lush, tropical island full of lovely bays and lagoons.

EXPLORING THE CORAL REEF

If you draw a line 2,000 miles straight south of Hawaii, you'll find a group of islands called French Polynesia. That's the destination of our dive trip. Our jet has just landed on Tahiti, the most famous island. We know some marine biologists from France who live 12 miles away on an island called Moorea. When we deplane, we assemble our gear and board a boat for Moorea. After the boat drops us off, we have to take a 35-minute bus ride to get to the biologists' research station. There we will stay for the next eight weeks.

The bus looks more like a truck. It rattles and bumps and has only two wooden benches on each side—the middle is used for luggage. But we don't mind because there's so much to see. The whole island is covered with tall coconut palms. The main road is lined with green bushes—my favorites are the hibiscus bushes, filled with brilliant red flowers.

The beautiful hibiscus is a common sight in the South Pacific.

The compressor, seen in the background, is driven by an engine similar to that in a lawnmower.

After our arrival at the research station, we unload our gear, renew acquaintances with old friends, and meet new ones. The next morning, we prepare for our first dive.

Only two of us will make this dive, and we each have special jobs to do to prepare for the dive. The underwater photographer's job is complex. For both an amphibious camera and a housed camera, the photographer must be certain that all the little rubber rings that seal the parts of the camera together are clean. Even one grain of sand will break the seal and allow water into the camera. The flash attachment, or *strobe,* is also sealed by a ring that must be cleaned. The large battery in the strobe is checked to see that it is working.

The tanks must also be filled. They are filled by a *compressor,* which takes air from the outside and forces it into the tank. Each tank takes about half an hour to fill.

While the tanks are being filled and photographic equipment is being checked, I check off and load the gear into the boat. Each of us has a tank, a regulator, mask, fins, snorkel, wetsuit, boots, a weight belt and a BC. One of us also has an underwater watch and a depth gauge. The camera gear is loaded last and put inside a towel so that it doesn't get damaged.

We decide on a dive spot that is 30 to 40 feet deep and drop anchor to keep the boat from drifting while we dive. Then we put on our gear. We attach our regulators to our tanks and turn on the air. We make sure our weight belts can be easily removed if necessary, put on our masks and fins, and we're ready. The photographer usually enters the water last so that he can hand his gear to a diver already in the water. Each of us enters the water from a small boat by sitting on the edge, putting one hand on our mask to keep the water from pulling it off, and falling gently backwards into the water. We put our regulators in our mouths and begin to submerge, clearing ours ears gently as we slowly descend.

To reach the barrier reef, the boat must be steered between coral heads that lie just below the surface.

41

Descending down the anchor line provides added safety in water that has a strong current or low visibility.

This is one of the most exciting parts of the dive. Looking into about 40 feet of water, our bodies float gently toward a coral reef teeming with life. We immediately check the anchor to be certain that it is wedged securely behind a piece of coral or a rock. The reef slowly comes into focus. Colored fish of all shapes and sizes swim through the coral. Tube worms that look like tiny colored Christmas tree lights pop out of the coral heads.

Above: Rudderfish find safety in the hard limestone formations of the reef. Below: Tube worms, with their brightly colored gills, live in the coral and use it for protection.

A multicolored handfish looks down from his coral perch like a judge about to pass sentence on a human intruder.

The clownfish swims unafraid among the poisonous tentacles of the sea anemone. Other fish that venture too close are suddenly paralyzed and, within seconds, become food for the anemone.

Like long, slender fingers, the sea anemone waves its tentacles in the current. A yellow fish, one foot long and one inch wide, swims by. It is appropriately named the trumpet fish.

We peer under a coral ledge and discover the butterfly cod fish. We don't touch it because the spines are poisonous. It's not aggressive, and it lets us look at its lovely long brown and white spines that look like whiskers, each waving independently in the current.

Accidently kicking the sand with my fin, I scare up a flounder—a flat, sand-colored fish. It's very shy and scuttles off as fast as it can, staying close to the bottom.

There's not much down here that can harm us because we respect and don't tease the sea creatures. The moray eel looks ferocious with its thick, snakelike body and row of teeth down the center of its mouth. We quietly watch the eel in its hole in the coral, and it does nothing more than peer out at us from the safety of its home.

The tropical waters of the world are home to a wide variety of beautifully colored fish.

A forest of coral is home for the smaller animals on the reef. Coral comes in all shapes and colors, and it's usually named for what it looks like. Staghorn coral is orange and thin and spiky, like the antlers of a deer. Brain coral is a grayish purple and is convoluted like a human brain. Pink tabletop coral has a stem and then becomes flat, like a table. The different coral formations provide small fish with hiding places from their enemies, and also make the reef a beautiful place to be.

When we reach our limit for a no-decompression dive, we begin our ascent to the surface. After we have helped each other off with our tanks and removed our masks, fins, weight belts and BCs, we start the engine on the boat. Only then do we pull up anchor, so the motor can keep us from drifting too close to the shallow part of the reef.

When we arrive back at the research station, we rinse off all our gear under an outdoor shower. We rinse ourselves off, too—a shower is refreshing after all that hard work. We hang our gear on a line to dry, and then we notice how hungry we are. Over lunch, we talk about all the wonders we have just seen.

CONCLUSION

Scuba diving is a unique sport that combines a feeling of competence and knowledge of underwater safety with the thrill of underwater exploration. Because human beings have been able to explore freely under water for only about 40 years, new discoveries in this special undersea world are always being made. The scuba diver sees a world that land-bound friends are unaware of. Sunlit reefs outline the eastern shores of many continents. And very deep down, bamboo coral emits its eerie blue light while, unheard by human ears, old sunken ships groan under the weight of the water. The possibilities for exploring this planet within a planet are limitless—but only if you can dive!

Superwheels & Thrill Sports

Airplanes
AEROBATICS
AIRPLANE RACING
FLYING-MODEL AIRPLANES
HELICOPTERS
HOME-BUILT AIRPLANES
PERSONAL AIRPLANES
SCALE-MODEL AIRPLANES
THE WORLD'S GREATEST AIRPLANES: I & II
YESTERDAY'S AIRPLANES

Automobiles & Auto Racing
AMERICAN RACE CAR DRIVERS
THE DAYTONA 500
DRAG RACING
ICE RACING
THE INDIANAPOLIS 500
INTERNATIONAL RACE CAR DRIVERS
LAND SPEED RECORD BREAKERS
RALLYING
ROAD RACING
TRACK RACING

CLASSIC SPORTS CARS
CUSTOM CARS
DINOSAUR CARS: LATE GREAT CARS
   FROM 1945 TO 1966

FABULOUS CARS OF THE 1920s & 1930s
KIT CARS: CARS YOU CAN BUILD YOURSELF
MODEL CARS
RESTORING YESTERDAY'S CARS
VANS: THE PERSONALITY VEHICLES
YESTERDAY'S CARS

Bicycles
BICYCLE ROAD RACING
BICYCLE TRACK RACING
BICYCLES ON PARADE

Motorcycles
GRAND NATIONAL CHAMPIONSHIP RACES
MOPEDS: THE GO-EVERYWHERE BIKES
MOTOCROSS MOTORCYCLE RACING
MOTORCYCLE RACING
MOTORCYCLES ON THE MOVE
THE WORLD'S BIGGEST MOTORCYCLE RACE:
   THE DAYTONA 200

Other Specialties
KARTING
MOUNTAIN CLIMBING
RIVER THRILL SPORTS
SAILBOAT RACING
SPORT DIVING
SKYDIVING
SNOWMOBILE RACING
YESTERDAY'S FIRE ENGINES
YESTERDAY'S TRAINS
YESTERDAY'S TRUCKS

Lerner Publications Company
241 First Avenue North, Minneapolis, Minnesota 55401